TAKE THE LULL BY THE HORNS!

CLOSING THE LEADERSHIP GAP

by

Lee E. Meadows, Ph.D

Bloomington, IN authorHOUSE® Milton Keynes, UK

AuthorHouse™
1663 Liberty Drive, Suite 200
Bloomington, IN 47403
www.authorhouse.com
Phone: 1-800-839-8640

AuthorHouse™ UK Ltd.
500 Avebury Boulevard
Central Milton Keynes, MK9 2BE
www.authorhouse.co.uk
Phone: 08001974150

First published by AuthorHouse 11/21/2006

ISBN: 978-1-4259-7932-4 (sc)
ISBN: 978-1-4259-7931-7 (hc)

Library of Congress Control Number: 2006910054

Printed in the United States of America
Bloomington, Indiana

This book is printed on acid-free paper.

TAKE THE LULL BY THE HORNS!

CLOSING THE LEADERSHIP GAP

Advance Praise for 'Take the Lull by the Horns!

"Does for leadership what "The Goal" did for productivity".

Art Espey, Chief Operating Officer
Power Process Piping, Inc

"An engaging story with valuable insight into leadership in the global economy. This book gave me hope! Innovation and creativity can thrive if employees are given the tools. Nothing Dull about the Lull!"

Dr. M. Kate Murphy,
Program Manager in Lifelong Education and
Professor of Speech
Washtenaw Community College

"Take the Lull by the Horns shows readers in a practical manner how to assess themselves so they can become more effective managers who make profitable and positive contributions to their organizations. There are scores of books and dozens of speakers today expounding the 'how to's' of understanding and managing other people. Unfortunately, there are few, if any, which focus on understanding and managing oneself."
Dr. Tom G. Javarinis
University Professor of Management
Director of Human Resources - Metro Health Services

"I liked the plot, the characters and the positive learning. The book would make a great workplace gift. Well done!"

Karla Kretzschmer
Human Resource Change Management Consultant
The Thomson Corporation

'Taking the Lull by the Horns' is a great quick and informative read that pointed out the fact that on several occasions' I have outright ignored or dismissed opportunities to grow professionally as a leader and improve my department's performance level. Lee Meadows has developed a well thought out way to stimulate people into lifting their heads out of the sand, and realize that the day-to-day grind of work can "lull" you into missing important facts and indicators by not paying close enough attention to environment.

Tarik Rashidi,
Director of Support Services
In-House Diagnostic Solutions

⤙ SPECIAL DEDICATION ⤚

*My family, Phyllis (my wife) and Garrison (my son)
To whom I can gratefully say, 'there's never a lull
moment!'*

⊷ DEDICATION ⊶

This book is dedicated to all of the students, managers, employees, leaders and friends who have allowed me the opportunity to spend quality 'educational' time with them. The debates, lectures, tirades and moments of transformative enlightenment were worth every moment spent in a vortex and every detour along the way.

"Lead it or Leave it"
Lee E. Meadows

⚜ ACKNOWLEDGEMENTS ⚜

Taking the lull by the horns speaks to the character and willingness of an individual to push their own creativity beyond institutional restrictions, toward that burst of light where unlimited opportunities reside. I have known, respected, and befriended several along the way.

Dr. Ernest Betts, Dean of Multicultural Programs for the College of Business at Michigan State University.

Patricia (Pat) Leonard, Vice Chancellor for Student Affairs at the University of North Carolina at Wilmington.

Dr. Phyllis Meadows, Director of Health and Wellness for the City of Detroit

Dr. Roger Newton, Senior Vice President of Pfizer Global Research and Development and Director of Esperion Therapeutics

Dr. Dave Odett, Vice President for Academic Affairs at Capitol College

Keith Pretty, President of Northwood University

Bringing this book to life could not have been accomplished without the special help of some very dedicated people who also happen to be wonderful graduate students at Walsh College

Regina Smith, thanks for the creative cover design.

Montez Clark, Shante Quinzy, Pete Sternisha and Alicia Washeleski, I am grateful for your valuable input during the final stages of this project.

Katereena Rashidi, your practical insights about the content were right on target.

⇌ CONTENTS ⇌

⇥ PREFACE ⇤

Over the thirty plus years that have shaped, crafted and sharpened the dull edges of my career, I have had the good fortune of meeting and working with some incredibly talented people. Their experiences in corporate, nonprofit, public, university and small business settings have provided focused insight on a common thread that has woven its way into the fabric of organizational life. Those experiences speak to unfulfilled opportunities that result from organizational or self-imposed restriction in the pursuit of creative, culture-shifting, and market-changing ideas.

Many of the conversations, told in private, centered on an inability to get their ideas heard, try new approaches or explore different ways to make a difference. While many are, rightfully, concerned about rocking the boat, they all have come to understand that it isn't the water that rocks the boat, but the motion of the ocean. Organizations can stagnate around time tested, comfortably safe ideas that don't move beyond the needs of a vanishing customer. Most employees can see what is going on around them, but resort to a form of organizational blindness in acting on what they see.

Take the Lull by the Horns captures the thread of those employee experiences and lays claim to the idea that the competitive marketplace can ill afford less than engaged players. The expanding global market demands fresh ideas, new approaches and that creative spark that sits at the core of human behavior. It's a journey in which I have seen some of the most profitable ideas come from employees who, once acknowledged, lit up the organizational universe like a bright star and reaffirmed their commitment to being something special, in a place where being special is celebrated.

⊷ INTRODUCTION ⊷

'*Take the Lull by the Horns!*' is a story about the business times of this still early 21ˢᵗ century. Business as usual is a sentiment that speaks to the past but also anchors us in the belief that the past reveals the future. Business couldn't be more unusual and the moxie needed to blaze forward is a far cry from the sweat and muscle of the preceding century.

People make the most difference and the unleashing of potential is the greatest competitive advantage afforded to any organization. Tucked somewhere in the back of a jumbled work cube is an employee wrestling with the next great idea, but it never comes forward because the events of the moment hinder future possibilities. This book is not about wait and see, but stand and deliver. What makes a business great is its ability to seize opportunities and turn them into great events. Sometimes that happens by luck, sometimes it happens by default, but for the 21st century, it will happen most often when we decide to stop waiting and move forward.

⊷ PRELUDE ⊷

Esprimtech grew out of the merger and acquisition decade of the 1980's. As a small, privately held company that specialized in software tech support, the company was a Wall Street darling through most of the 1980's and most of the 1990's. The company was founded by three close friends who'd grown up together in Detroit and after having spent a number of years being software support specialist for different Detroit-based companies, decided to cash in their stock options and 401k plans, secure financing from several venture capitalist and create Esprimtech. The twenty-two level, glass towered structure symbolized a revitalized downtown and represented the birth of the other industry that would compliment the long established and internationally known automotive industry. Esprimtech landed its first big contract as a supplier with the larger of the automotive giants and from there its reputation grew from local and regional accolades, to positive mention in business journals from coast to coast. The founders became part of the corporate elite. As first generation, new money multi-millionaires, their names were frequently mentioned in the same breath as their Silicon Valley contemporaries. Esprimtech's ten thousand highly talented and credentialed employees came from the best local, national and international universities. They were given the most barrier free work environment, top salaries and benefits and an annual 'Thank You' party that was sponsored by the company and held on one of the Caribbean Islands. Things had gone so well within the company that little attention was paid to globalization and the subsequent outsourcing that came with companies finding less expensive ways to maintain their tech support. Along the way, Esprimtech lost several major contracts and stopped funding many of its R & D activities. The company had gone into a survival mode and searched for ways to cut costs while still generating more business. The company needed to look to new markets, different clients and competitive pricing in order to maintain a slight hold on its market share. Other competitors sensed Esprimtech's vulnerability and immediately went after many of its former clients. The company was in a tailspin and needed to do something before it crashed.

⟫ CHAPTER 1 ⟪

Sam Brown managed to stay just below the speed limit as he wove in and around the stop and start movement of late afternoon commuter traffic. He reasoned that he'd only be a few minutes late for his evening graduate class. He had taken a few minutes to glance over the chapter readings and knew if called upon, he had enough information to at least give the illusion of knowing something. However, it was the discussion that took place in an earlier emergency meeting that swirled around in his head.

In two months, there had been six emergency meetings, each more intense than the previous, but all with a common theme. Profits were down. Sales were down. The stock was in a downward spiral and another round of layoffs was imminent. Throughout the turmoil, Sam's position as the Manager of

Strategic Initiatives hadn't been placed on the chopping block, but it didn't minimize the constant ache he felt in the back of his neck.

"How am I supposed to get it all done when I'll be minus three more staff members?" he asked while listening to the I-75 northbound traffic report. It was the same question he asked his Director, Cindy Mitchell, earlier at the emergency staff meeting. Her answer had gained pop culture status within the company as the most unoriginal response to an emotionally tense situation.

"You'll just have to find a way," Cindy had replied for the sixth straight time in sixth straight emergency meeting.

"I'll just have to find a way. Yeah, right," Sam muttered as he eased onto the exit ramp. If he was lucky enough to find a good parking spot, he'd make it to class with a couple of minutes to spare.

Sam grabbed his briefcase from the passenger seat, hit the button on his remote to lock the car doors and raced into the one story building. He was moving down the carpeted hallway toward class when he spotted his instructor, Dr. Angela Patterson, walking toward him. He began to slow down once he realized that her presence outside of the class meant that he had the unexpected gift of a few extra minutes of breathing time.

"Good evening, Dr. Patterson," Sam said.

"Sam," she replied. "What brings you here tonight?"

Sam smiled and said, "Nice try, Dr. Patterson, but you know I'm here for your class."

Dr. Patterson smiled. "Well, Sam, it looks like one of us is one day ahead of our normal class meeting time."

Sam stopped mid-step, looked at Dr. Patterson and furrowed his forehead. "Don't we have class tonight?"

"Not unless the class decided to move it from Wednesday to Tuesday and I wasn't informed." She replied.

Sam smacked his forehead realizing what happened. "Today is Tuesday...isn't it?"

"Somehow, I believe the statement, 'Yep, all day', would not be seen as a humorous punch line right now, so why don't I just admit that it's Tuesday and ask if you're having another bad day."

"Not another bad day," Sam said as he leaned back against the wall. "It's a continuation of the one that started two months ago."

"I'm headed back to my office to return a phone call. If you'd like to come along, I'd be happy to talk with you about whatever's on your mind."

"Thanks, Dr. Patterson, but as much as I appreciate the concern, I'm well aware of the 'would you like cheese with that whine?' sarcasm currently making the rounds within the student culture."

"Don't worry about that. You would hardly qualify as a whiner. They have a different glow about them."

As they walked back to her office, Dr Patterson listened as Sam talked about the events that were reshaping his place of work and the most recent staff meeting. "And her comment to me was 'You'll just have to find a way', like that's supposed to help me figure out how I'm going to get the work of three people out of one person."

"Sam, did it ever occur to you that maybe what you heard her say is not what she really said?"

"Dr. Patterson, I heard exactly what she said." Sam replied politely.

"I don't doubt the accuracy of what you heard, what I'm asking you to do is think about the content, the meaning and substance of what was said."

"The meaning was clear. We have to do more with less."

"Yes, Sam, that is one meaning, but did you also hear the leadership focus?"

"I don't think she's leading at all."

"She may not be, then again maybe she's being a good leader in response to a volatile climate in which she is creating an opportunity for you and others to show creative initiative. I call it *take the lull by the horns*."

"Take the lull by the horns?"

Stopping in front of her office door, Dr. Patterson said. "I use that phrase as a way of distinguishing leaders who don't scream that the 'sky is falling', but notice that the sky is falling and search for ways to return it to its glory."

"Dr. Patterson, with all due respect, there is nothing glorious about the sky falling."

"It is if it reveals to you things that you didn't know were there. Take the lull by the horns is just another way of trying to get at something that was previously hidden to you. It's knowing that the answer to the falling sky problem is not a matter of running to avoid being hit, but standing still to see what lands in front of and around you."

"But, that doesn't make any..."

"I'll tell you what, Sam. Let me return this urgent phone call and we'll talk about it when I'm done. Meantime, the faculty lounge is vacant right now. Why don't you go and pour yourself a cup of coffee, have a seat and I'll come and get you when I'm done."

Sam nodded and slowly made his way to the faculty lounge area. The room contained a wall of mail slots, two copy machines, a counter with a sink, a recently carpeted floor as well as a black leather three person couch backed against a corner wall. He noticed that the brewed coffee had been sitting for a while, sighed, walked over to the empty couch and melted into the corner, leaning against an arm rest.

"How does one *take the lull by the horns?*" he muttered while trying to stifle a yawn.

✤ CHAPTER 2 ✤

"That's a good question, Sam. Would you care to explore some answers?"

Sam suddenly realized that he was standing outside of the downtown office building of Esprimtech, face to face with Dr. Patterson.

"What are we doing here?" he asked.

"I thought we'd go back over your day. I noticed a few leadership opportunities that you let slip by."

"But, how could you have…?

"They were the kind of opportunities that will make a difference in both the short and long term."

She led him across the marble plated floor of the cavernous lobby to the waiting elevator.

"Wait, I didn't show my ID and you didn't sign in."

Dr. Patterson nodded toward the elevator and asked. "Do you remember the conversation you had with Janelle Stewart this morning while you two were riding in this elevator?"

Two years out of her MBA program and ready to take on the world, Janelle Stewart was a twenty-five year old Marketing Manager assigned to Sam's project team. Identified as a 'fast tracker' from the moment she was hired, she moved quickly to network with the right people, lobbied to be placed on high profile assignments and worked hard to be seen doing the 'right' things. Janelle was standing in front of the elevator wearing the same navy blue pant suit Sam had noticed that morning.

"I remember hearing her complain about how she wasn't being promoted fast enough." Sam said. "I took it as youthful impatience and told her to lighten up, put in your time and to try not to say anything stupid."

"She must have found that conversation to be very inspirational?"

"It was early and I wasn't in the mood for her morning tirade." As they walked toward the elevator, Sam asked. "Am I going to have to hear this conversation again?"

"No, but I do want to show you something?" Dr. Patterson responded.

As they stood poised outside of Janelle's cubicle, Sam said, "Wait a minute. How did you...?

Dr. Patterson pointed to Janelle's computer screen. "Look at what she's doing."

Janelle was searching the internet looking at various corporate websites.

"Great, she's conducting research on our competitors. I gave her that assignment as part of our project."

"Look closer," Dr. Patterson said.

Sam leaned over Janelle's shoulder and saw that she was researching a competitors' website and specifically looking at job postings. Janelle read a job description, clicked on the Human Resource link and uploaded a resume.

"She wants to leave the company?" Sam asked.

"So, it would seem."

"But, she's being fast tracked here."

"Yes, she's being surfed around the company, but there's no substance to her assignments."

Dr. Patterson went on to explain how youth and experience are incompatible roommates and that the patience and sacrifice that shaped the career lives of previous generations don't carry the same weight with employees like Janelle. Oftentimes, an impatient leap will blind these kinds of employees to the underlying and peripheral career possibilities that could add both breadth and depth. "Your company may use the influence of its culture and policies to suppress Janelle's impatience, but also realize it's that same impatience that has spawned a generation of first-time multi-millionaire entrepreneurs."

"I can't alter my project to accommodate her impatience. Besides, why should I worry about something that her manager should be addressing?"

"What she shared with you this morning was not about getting formal advice, but informal guidance. You are a member of the same company and, by extension, an agent of your company's mission and commitment to its employees. You don't have to be her boss to give guidance. You only needed to listen to her concerns and channel her obvious drive into something that would be beneficial to both her and the company. She wasn't complaining out of frustration, she was asking for opportunities to lead."

"If she wants to lead, she can take over my project. I have too much to do as it is."

Dr. Patterson smiled.

"Why are you smiling like that?" Sam asked. "You're not suggesting that I actually turn over responsibility for my project to some kid who is looking to set the world on fire but doesn't have a clue as to how to light a match?"

Dr. Patterson continued smiling.

"Do you realize the impact of that kind of decision? I would be hung out to dry for neglecting my responsibilities."

"You would not be giving up authority for the project, just delegating the day-to-day leadership responsibilities to someone who is eager to learn. Your new found leadership role would be to guide, counsel and develop Janelle's leadership skills while still retaining key input to bring the project to completion."

"It would cause a lot of disruption...

"That would easily settle down within a meeting or two," Dr. Patterson stated.

"Are you saying I should try it?" Sam asked.

"I'm saying you should think about it," Dr. Patterson replied.

Dr. Patterson watched as Sam wrestled with the merits of transitioning his project leadership responsibilities to someone not as tested and for whom he had no direct managerial responsibility. She didn't expect him to embrace the idea without some reluctance and concern. It wouldn't be the first time she'd helped someone work through the idea of delegating leadership responsibility. Sam typified many of the managers she'd help develop through her consulting practice. As a leadership coach, Dr. Patterson recognized that managers like Sam found their leadership muscle through the traditional 'Baptism by Fire' strategy. While this method may well have demonstrated to the organization those persons capable of weathering the storm, the higher levels of burnout, disenchantment and minimalist creativity only created a bigger gap between the organization's present capability and its future leadership needs.

Dr. Patterson had remarked to a group of Manufacturing Managers:

"It is difficult to swim toward the island when you are barely staying afloat."

All effort has to be goal-directed or it becomes a futile waste of energy and time.

Dr Patterson tapped Sam on the shoulder and said: "Sam, let me show you something." She pointed to the ceiling above Janelle's cubicle. Sam looked up and read:

+ Immediate, short term leadership strategies are thinly veiled panic attacks.
+ Reacting to the 'now' satisfies the hunger, but does little to expand the appetite.
+ Fighting off the wolves at the front door leaves you vulnerable to the coyotes in the back.
+ Planning for the future is difficult if you continue to prioritize the past.

Sam said, "Okay, I'll give it serious thought, but…

"Not now, Sam." Dr. Patterson replied. "Let's move on."

⇥ CHAPTER 3 ⇤

Sam and Dr. Patterson were standing outside of Conference Room 'A' watching as a group of employees eased through the door and sat in the leather back chairs to wait for the meeting to start.

"Do you remember what happened at this morning's meeting?" Dr. Patterson asked.

Sam shook his head and replied, "I sure do. What a waste of time." He nodded toward the group of people sitting at the conference table. "You'll notice that half of them haven't arrived. The meeting was supposed to start ten minutes ago."

"Why didn't it start on time?"

"Frank Jordan, the Purchasing Manager and team leader never starts the meeting on time because he's never there on time."

"But, you were on time."

"Yes, I was on time, but it wasn't my meeting."

"Whose meeting was it?"

"I just told you it was Frank's meeting."

"Well, look around the room and tell me what you see."

Sam noticed that several of those in attendance had their laptops open and were answering email, surfing the net or playing Solitaire. One team member spent most of his time drawing pictures of horses. Despite his frustration with the late starting time, he had remained calm enough and kind enough to place a sketch of Frank's head on the front end of one of his horse drawings. A strained politeness masked most of the informal conversation and after checking their watches several times, Frank finally made an appearance, apologizing for being late and out of breath.

"Why did you roll your eyes when he apologized?" Dr. Patterson asked.

"His apology is so standard and trite that I don't give it much weight, plus," Sam paused. "You have got to hear where he spends the first ten minutes of an already late meeting."

Dr. Patterson smiled knowing what was about to happen.

Frank's apology was immediately followed by a blow-by-blow account of his pending divorce. He talked about the burdensome shift in lifestyle, his changing role with his children and how his soon-to-be-ex-wife was making the transition even more difficult. Frank's divorce trauma had become part unofficial 'therapy session' that preceded the actual team meeting. The last five team members that wandered in breathed a sigh of relief knowing they'd missed being part of Frank's therapeutic support on company time.

"So, now that the meeting has started late, it will end late which means that all of us will have to alter our already jammed schedules and roll back the starting times of other meetings we may have planned."

"Here's something else you might want to think about," Dr Patterson said. "Based on my speculation of the salaries of the individuals sitting in this room, breaking it down into an hourly rate and multiplying that number by what I believe will be two wasted hours, your company has just spent about thirty thousand dollars for a meeting that never took place."

"So, Frank is not only wasting our time, but he's also wasting company money."

"Well, if you see it as Frank's meeting, then, yes, that would be true." Dr. Patterson replied.

"Whose meeting is it? Sam asked.

"I asked you first,"

Sam paused.

Dr. Patterson used the moment to reflect on a seminar she delivered to a group of corporate IT staff members where she pointed out that team leaders often fail to realize that the gathering of expertise inside a corporate setting to work on a specific project is, essentially, about the effective use that paid talent's time. She reminded the group that holding meetings is an essential tool for gathering valuable input, solving problems and making decisions about on-going concerns. The team leader has to be committed to making sure that the team is the best compilation of talent needed for the task and the use of the talent occurs in a timely manner.

"I guess from a 'big picture' perspective the meeting really belongs to everyone in that room." Sam stated.

"From that perspective, you're right."

"And, I suppose there's no law that says we have to wait for Frank. There are a number of tasks that can be discussed and completed without him having to be there."

"All it requires is someone willing to step into the leadership void and push the agenda forward."

"Well, that's part of the problem. We don't usually *have* an agenda." Sam stated

"Which also validates my point," Dr Patterson stated.

"The only downside to your point is that when it comes time to assign credit for having completed the project, Frank will receive an undue amount while the real team members will receive very little."

"Frank will only receive what he deserves." Dr. Patterson stated. "Meanwhile, the organization will receive the full benefit of an unintended leadership experience that will only be seen as successful."

"You're saying I should have stepped in and moved the meeting along despite Frank's consistent lateness."

"You had a clear opportunity to lead by example in the truest sense of the statement." She pointed to the white board where Sam read:

- Every meeting should be an opportunity to effectively use time, not waste the company's most irrevocable resource
- Call a meeting, solve a problem
- The only good meeting is a good meeting
- Start on time, end on time all the time
- Have an agenda with the coffee and doughnuts

Dr Patterson said, "Don't take cover behind Frank's personal traumas; take strength in leading the group toward completion."

"So far, it looks like my day could have been a lot busier."

"I'd like to think it could have been more enlightening, but we're only just beginning."

↽ CHAPTER 4 ⇀

Sam stood on the stairwell that was one level above his work area staring down at Francis McCullough as she made her way up the stairs. She was completing the last week of her internship and, as Sam had observed earlier, she also seemed upset.

"Do you remember passing her earlier today?" Dr. Patterson asked.

"Barely," Sam replied. "I was in a hurry to meet with the Facilities Manager. I do remember asking her if something was wrong. She said 'No!'"

"You believed her?"

"No, not really, but I was in a hurry and didn't have time to listen to her problems."

"Well, let's see if we can decipher her problem."

As they stood outside the office of the Facilities Manager, Sam and Dr. Patterson were able to overhear the conversation that took place between Francis and Doug Lewis. Having never had to work with an intern during his time as a Facilities Manager, Doug had never been comfortable with how Francis had befriended the Human Resources Manager at a local conference and used that relationship to land an internship with his department. During her fourteen weeks, Doug had only given her assignments that basically kept her out of his way and required very little skill. Sam recalled a few occasions when Francis was seen knocking on someone's cube wall, smiling and asking if there was anything they needed.

"I always thought she was being proactive." Sam stated.

"She was looking for something to do." Dr. Patterson replied.

Sam listened as Doug completed his conversation with Francis.

Doug said, "So, I hope all went well and that this internship *you* wanted was a good experience."

"Somehow, I always thought there was more to facilities management than what I experienced. I went after this internship with this company because I hope to be a Facilities Manager one day," Francis replied

"Well, that's a long way off and a lot of things can happen between now and then." Doug said while checking a flow chart on his computer screen.

"Will it be okay for me to use you as a reference?"

"Yes, I'll be happy to confirm that you had an internship here."

Francis stood up and said. "Then I want to thank you for all that you've done. I'll make sure my remaining assignments are completed before I finish out the week."

Doug nodded, never taking his eyes off the computer screen.

"No wonder she was upset," Sam said.

Every effort Francis made to gloss over the fact that nothing was wrong only made it more apparent. She walked past her cubicle and took the exit to the stairwell. She hesitated before starting up the stairs. She leaned against the metal rail, trying to collect her thoughts before hurrying to her next meeting.

"This must have been when I came running by," Sam said.

"Do you understand what happened between Francis and Doug?" Dr. Patterson asked.

"Well, granted, he wasn't exactly supportive," Sam responded.

Dr. Patterson smiled and pointed to Doug' computer screen. "Walk around and see what's on the web page he's reading?"

Sam walked around the desk and stood behind Doug's chair. He glanced over Doug's right shoulder and read the information on the web page.

- ✦ Leaders see potential, not problems
- ✦ Every interaction is filled with promise
- ✦ Missed opportunities are more abundant
- ✦ Believe it, then you'll see it

Sam said, "I thought he was reading a facilities report."

"He is," Dr. Patterson replied. "The information you're reading is for you."

"But, he was the one that blew the chance to positively impact her career, right?"

"Yes, but he wasn't the only one."

"Okay, then I'll find time to get with her tomorrow," Sam stated.

"Don't bother, Sam, she won't be in tomorrow," Dr Patterson said. "You see, the manager from a previous internship has been trying to reach her to offer her a full time job. He encouraged her to try another experience before he'd offer her anything. Now, that she's had a sample of leadership in your company, she's made the comparison and decided to go where her potential can be realized."

"I didn't realize the day had been filled with so many things that could have turned out better than they started." Sam said.

Dr. Patterson put her hand on Sam's shoulder, "Let's take a walk."

⇥ CHAPTER 5 ⇤

Outside of the building, the company had built a combination exercise trail and recreational area for employees to use during their free moments. Sam followed Dr. Patterson as she led him toward a row of tables that were comfortably designed for employees who wanted to enjoy their lunch in the open air. Dr. Patterson pointed to a silver-haired, burly gentleman dining alone at one end of a table. He nervously tapped his fingers on the table top while sipping his beverage from its plastic cup.

"Now, wait a second," Sam said. "I distinctly remember my conversation with Anton and there was nothing significant about it. There was no missed leadership opportunity."

"What did you talk about?" Dr. Patterson asked.

"Well, he did most of the talking and it essentially covered his hope that once we come through this economic crisis, things will go back to the way they were. You know, he started with the company right out of high school. He came in at a time when the company practically guaranteed cradle to grave lifetime employment. He's seen the company through its good times and now its bad times. I agreed with him."

"Agreed with what?"

"I agreed that the company was going through some rough times. I agreed that the company will come through it. I agreed that when it happens, things will go back to the way they were."

"Remember the woman you were engaged to after you finished college?"

Stunned, Sam asked, "How did you know about her?"

"It was a great relationship wasn't it?"

"At the time, yeah, it was a great relationship. We started dating during our sophomore year and stayed in the relationship long after college. I'd given her an engagement ring."

"But, something happened?"

"Yeah, she got a great job with a company. She had to travel a lot, sometimes for weeks at a time. After six months, she was relocated to Cleveland. I was working for another company at the time. The long distance thing wasn't working. We were starting to drift apart. Finally we decided that I should move to Cleveland so we could be together. I packed up, moved to Cleveland believing that it would help put the relationship back on solid ground."

"Did it work?"

"Maybe for the first couple of weeks, but in time I realized that she had changed and, I guess, so had I. It was a strain to be together. She had made new friends and truly loved being a single woman in the big city. We were together physically, but emotionally distanced."

"I don't understand," Dr. Patterson said. "Hadn't things gone back to the way they were?"

"How could things go back to the way they were?" Sam asked. "A lot happened during that time and...."

Dr. Patterson smiled.

"And, a lot's happened to this company during this crisis, hasn't it?"

"Sometimes more than we care to admit." Dr. Patterson said.

"So, with Anton, what I should have said is that there is no way the company can go back to the way things were. A lot has happened."

Dr. Patterson explained to Sam how the global changes that affected his company, and others, had a profound impact on the internal way of life these companies had fostered for years. Cradle to grave lifetime employment was a luxury granted during a time of economic, domestic and international dominance. Thousands of employees like Anton came to work at a time when competition was neighborly and the rules were flexible. In order for things to go back to the way they were, the competition would have to stop being global, the economy would have to be tied to domestic productivity, consumers would have to return to being brand loyal, and there can only be three major television networks.

"Now, what's the likelihood of that occurring?" Dr. Patterson asked.

"It is about as likely as my getting an A+ in your Global Economics course."

"We have mutual agreement on that one."

"So, I should have told Anton to 'get real and wake up and smell the coffee.'"

"I think you could have given him a series of questions to think about. Oftentimes leadership isn't about providing answers, but asking questions for others to answer."

"What kinds of questions?"

Dr. Patterson pointed to the wooden sign posted at the first stop on the exercise trail. Sam glanced over and read:

+ **Are pleasant memories of the past pleasant for everyone?** *(Institutional memory is jaded. Those for whom it was favorable are still there and are living the glory days)*
+ **What needs to happen for you to get on board today?**
+ **What do you really fear about change?**
+ **Can you try something new?**

"You know, now that I think about it. I guess I could have mentioned to Anton that maybe he should start thinking of his career as less cradle to grave lifetime employment, but cubicle to cubicle lifelong learning."

"Come along, Sam, the fun is just beginning." Dr. Patterson said.

⊷ CHAPTER 6 ⊶

"Do you remember what you were doing at this time?" Dr. Patterson asked Sam.

Sam saw himself sitting in his office leafing through several pieces of paper single stacked in a green folder. He read one page, shook his head and then moved on to another. He repeated the pattern until he'd read every sheet of paper, closed the folder, leaned back in his chair and closed his eyes.

"I was reading a performance evaluation," Sam replied.

"Judging by the way you are leaned back in your chair, I'd say it was pretty dull reading."

"It's not the reading. It's the inevitable outcome. I'll probably have to fire this employee."

"Why?" Dr. Patterson asked.

Sam went on to explain how the employee had missed on several assignments over the last year. The quality of the completed assignments was questionable. As much as he'd tried to coach and develop the employee, it just wasn't working out.

"And on top of all that, the employee was a bit weird for the culture of this company." Sam said.

"What do you mean weird?"

"Weird, you know. The odd kind of character who doesn't really fit in."

Dr. Patterson walked over to Sam's desk and tapped the space bar on Sam's keyboard. The swimming fish screen saver vanished and another picture filled the flat screen monitor. Dr. Patterson nodded toward the screen. "Does this person look familiar?"

Sam squinted at the screen, paused and then smiled. "Sure, that's Mrs. Kirk, my seventh grade American History teacher. How did you...?

"Focus, Sam. What do you remember about her?"

"She was an odd character."

"What was odd about her?"

"She had this way of teaching that was way out of the box. She wouldn't just lecture; she was always asking questions to get us to think about our answers."

"That would make a lot of teachers odd," Dr. Patterson stated.

"It wasn't just that, but the other things she did. She would come to school dressed in the costume of an event we were studying. She'd walk around in that costume all day and have us act out characters. She would always ask, "What do you think the person would say? We were forced to make up something since we didn't really know what the character said."

"Sam, it sounds like it was a lot of fun."

"Yeah, it was okay. There was this one time when she asked me to figure out what John Paul Jones said after his famous statement, 'I have not yet begun to fight.' One of the students stood up, pretending to be a British Naval Captain and said, "Then, sir, prepare to die.""

"What did you believe John Paul Jones said after that comment?"

"Bring it on!"

Sam told more stories about Mrs. Kirk's odd behavior, frequently smiling or laughing at some of the things she did. "You know, she once did a talk on Symbolism and Reality by using the painting of George Washington standing up in the boat as he is crossing the Delaware River. She had us look at the painting and try to connect its symbolic meaning. She also dressed up like George Washington and stood in the exact pose as the one in the picture."

"What was the symbolism versus the reality?"

"Well, the reality is, he probably wasn't standing up because it was cold and the river currents were rough. Symbolically, that leadership pose was inspirational and a reflection of an important time."

"It's funny how years later, you still remember that lesson."

"I'm surprised that I still remember her." Sam paused, shook his head and smiled. "She was quite an odd duck, didn't really fit in, but she was some kind of teacher."

"It seems to me I've heard that word 'odd' rather recently."

"I'm missing something with this employee…right?"

"Read the page coming out of your printer," Dr. Patterson

Sam pulled the printed sheet from its tray and read the content

- Every successful business was started by an odd person with an idea
- Conform, yes, Contain, no
- Musicians and athletes know that its all about performance
- Don't whittle it down, wind it up and get out of the way

Sam said. "I guess how we view people really does depend on your point of view."

"Points of view are like waistlines, Sam. They can be broadened or narrowed. It's really up to the person."

"All this time, I thought Mrs. Kirk was crazy."

"She was, but that's beside the point," Dr. Patterson said. "Let's move on."

CHAPTER 7

The intercom buzzed twice, pulling Sam out his daze. He placed the green folder on his desk and removed the phone from its cradle.

"Do you remember this phone call?" Dr. Patterson asked.

Sam watched himself straddle the phone on his left shoulder and then spoke into the mouthpiece. "Yeah, it's Debbie from purchasing calling," Sam replied. "Let's go. From what I remember, this was a pretty dull conversation."

"Was it?"

Sam paused, "Don't tell me there was something I missed here."

"What do you think?"

"Now, look Dr. Patterson. I'm beginning to see your point about missed leadership opportunities, but this was just a purchasing conversation and nothing more."

"Well, let's listen in and see if it was about purchasing and nothing more."

Though Sam could see himself with the phone's receiver in his left ear, Debbie's voice came through on the intercom speaker.

"Wait a minute. You and I can hear the conversation on the intercom speaker, but the **me** that was actually having this conversation can't? That doesn't make…"

"Shush, Sam, just listen." Dr. Patterson said.

Sam watched as he rolled his eyes, leaned back in his chair and stared at the ceiling.

"And, observe," Dr. Patterson added.

Debbie's monologue centered on Sam's requisition for additional equipment to support his team's graphic and media needs. She requested additional information about the specific request to the muffled sounds of paper shuffling and the constant opening and closing of a desk drawer. Whenever she'd ask Sam a question, she would interrupt by asking him to 'hold on' while she checked another source.

"She was driving me crazy," Sam stated.

"Yes, had you bit your lip any harder the swelling would have qualified you as a male model for lip enhancement."

"She was taking too long to get to the point. Now how is that a missed leadership opportunity?"

"Give it another minute, Sam. I think it will become clear."

Sam focused less on how he had listened to her and began to listen as if hearing her for the first time.

"Sometimes, I don't understand how decisions are made around here. After all, if they want to get this purchasing process under control, then someone needs to figure out a way to pull together a better plan. Our transactions costs are not in line with the industry average and there is too much discretionary authority in manager's purchasing power. Most of them have never balanced a budget, correctly, and since they don't really see the money being spent, they spend as if it's a bottomless pit."

Sam turned toward Dr. Patterson. "I don't remember her saying anything like that."

"No wonder, Sam. Look at what you're doing."

Sam saw how he had spent the duration of the conversation staring at the ceiling, looking out the window, checking his cell phone for messages and moving items around on his desk. "I didn't realize I was that distracted, but you have to admit it's hard to stay in a long conversation with her and remain interested."

The phone conversation ended with Sam thanking Debbie for her help. He checked the clock on his computer screen and began opening up a file.

Dr. Patterson waited, while Sam thought about what he observed in his phone interaction with Debbie.

He finally broke the silence. "The conversation really wasn't about my purchasing request, was it?"

Dr. Patterson smiled and remained silent.

"I get it now. She was really trying to get help for a bigger problem she was having."

"I'd say it was more encouragement than help." Dr. Patterson stated. "I think she was using the conversation with you as a way of trying to solicit support for an idea she knows the organization desperately needs, but she wasn't quite sure how to go about making it happen."

"Why run it by me?"

"Maybe she respects your time with the company and your insight about how to get things done." Dr. Patterson paused and asked. "Now that you know what she really wanted, what could you have done differently?"

"But, I have no idea how to reorganize purchasing."

Dr. Patterson sighed. "What could you have done differently, Sam?"

"I suppose I could have given her some ideas on how to get her ideas heard." Sam lamented. "I could have told her that it's not ideas that get organizations excited, but how an idea can benefit the company."

"Sounds like Debbie already has a beneficial idea, she just needed an objective sounding board and a little encouragement on how to make it happen."

"Okay, so I blew that one, too. How am I supposed to know...?

"Sam," Dr. Patterson interrupted. "Look at your computer screen."

Sam turned toward the computer and watched as he opened another file.

Sam was astonished to see words roll across the screen as if sent by a power point application. "Wait a minute. That's not what I was looking at earlier."

"Read it, Sam."

- ◆ People will try new ideas or new organizations
- ◆ Missed opportunities bounce along until they find an open mind
- ◆ Hundreds of little ideas are worth more than one big idea
- ◆ Encouragement and guidance, the beginning of wisdom

"You know, Dr. Patterson. This stuff is becoming increasingly hard to believe.

"It will get easier. Let's go to lunch."

⇥ CHAPTER 8 ⇤

Outside the entrance to the company cafeteria, Dr. Patterson and Sam watched as employees slowly eased their way into the spacious room, glancing at each serving area as if they were indifferent to the nutritional offerings. The once noisy cafeteria was now a quiet reflection of the changes that had affected the company. The long finely polished tables that were once crowded with departments having a sit – down – brainstorming – lunch – group – bonding, were now long corners where two or three people gathered to commiserate about the latest group of employees to walk down the 'Pink Slip Runway'.

"Not very busy in here", Dr Patterson remarked.

"Most people are afraid to be seen eating lunch in the cafeteria for fear it will be perceived as not having enough to do." Sam said as he reflected on the busier, high noise level times of the cafeteria. "They've even outsourced the cafeteria service."

Dr. Patterson glanced around the cafeteria until she spotted an employee sitting alone at the farthest end of the cafeteria. His face was partially covered by the screen of his laptop. She tapped Sam on the arm to get his attention and pointed toward the corner.

"Oh no, not him." He said.

"I see you're not very fond of this person."

"His name is Aaron Scott and besides being an arrogant little snit, he's a boil on the butt of the organization."

"Well, there are surgical procedures for removing boils, but let's go see what he is doing."

They walked over to Aaron's table and watched as he feverishly fingered the keyboard, talked on his cell phone and consumed a large salad. Aaron, nodded, spoke in short sentences, sighed heavily and smacked his lips just loud enough to be heard by someone sitting across from him.

"I hate when he does that," Sam remarked. "He does that smacking sound and all that crazy keyboarding every time we're in a meeting together."

"What do you mean?" Dr. Patterson asked.

Sam explained how Aaron never seemed attentive in their meetings together. He was always pounding away on his laptop key board, his eyes almost never leaving the screen. The few times Sam had actually sat next to Aaron, he heard the sound of lips smacking. Aaron's manager, Margaret Donner, had confronted Aaron a number of times about his lack of attentiveness to the conversation taking place in the meetings.

"What was his response?"

"He'd just smack his lips and keep on keyboarding." Sam said as he mocked the smacking of lips.

"Now, it's my understanding that you had an opportunity to bring Aaron over to your group."

"How did you know that?" Sam asked.

"Is it true or not?" Dr. Patterson asked.

"Yes, as a matter of fact he approached me about a possible transfer. I told him I'd think about and get back with him."

"Which really means....?"

"He can keep on being Margaret's problem."

Sam went on to talk about Aaron's reputation throughout the company. Aaron's behavior had annoyed a number of people around the building. He has a technical expertise the company needs as it moves through the difficult times, so he was tolerated for what he brought to the table.

"The mere fact that he is an annoyance at the table is overlooked because of what he can do." Sam said.

"Did you ever think about why he approached you about a transfer?"

"No, but I know Margaret wouldn't block the transfer if I pursued it."

"Perhaps Aaron's developmental needs aren't consistent with what Margaret can provide."

"So?"

Dr. Patterson smiled, shook her head and thought of the number of Managers she'd met and trained over the years that, invariably, made the same remark after hearing a statement they hadn't considered. "So, maybe during those moments of lip smacking inattentiveness, he sensed something in you that he needed."

Sam looked around the cafeteria. The lightly whispered conversations and poker-faced responses from the various patrons seemed more than just surface defenses against the changes that were taking place. There was something deeper, more concrete and desperate than what he'd known. "They all need something, don't they?"

"Instability, uncertainty, and unpredictability are the Three Musketeers of organizational change. They force needs to the surface. We move to satisfy those needs and until we can, our behavior can suffer in other areas. Aaron may be a royal pain…."

"Aaron *IS* a royal pain," Sam interrupted.

"Yes, he is a royal pain, but much of pain can be minimized if he's aligned with the right person at this critical point in his career."

"The idea of having Aaron report to me gives me a royal pain."

"It wouldn't be the first time an employee experiencing failure in one department finds success in another and under a different style of leadership."

"But, what about…?

"Sam, read what's written on the tabletop next to Aaron's laptop."

Sam stared at the glowing yellow words that appeared on the table.

- ◆ Leaders find a way
- ◆ 90 percent of what is natural, is developed through experience
- ◆ A slight turn can be just as powerful as a 180 degree swing
- ◆ Listen to what's being asked, respond to what's needed

"Hmmm," Sam muttered. "I hadn't thought about it like that."

"I'm glad you enjoyed your lunch. Let's go." Dr. Patterson said.

⇥ Chapter 9 ⇤

Sam and Dr. Patterson stood outside the office of Laurel Manning, the Director of Global Business and listened while she threw a tirade in front of her four direct reports. They had gathered around a conference table in her windowed, corner office and listened while she angrily expressed her disappointment with the lack of sales performance in their designated global markets.

"These walls are soundproof. How is it that we can hear…?"

"Just listen, Sam." Dr Patterson said.

"It's not that I want you all to think outside of the box," Laurel was heard to say. I'd be happy if you just moved from the center of the box to a particular corner and hung out there for a while."

Laurel's four staff members sat idly, hoping her anger would subside so they could explain why global sales had not gone as well as expected.

Laurel continued, "Is there anyone here unfamiliar with the concept of quarterly earnings?"

The staff members nodded assuring her that they were more than familiar with quarterly earnings.

"Good," she said, "Then, explain to me why the earnings we projected for this quarter are being met?"

"I know the answer to that question," Sam offered.

"I suspect that they know the answer to, Sam." Dr. Patterson stated. "Keep listening."

Sam listened as Laurel continued to rant about the missed projections, the lack of initiative on their part, their inability to perform their jobs and her spiritual question of wanting to know why she was burdened with such an incompetent staff.

"Your performance is unacceptable and I won't put up with it much longer." Laurel said as she sat down at the head of the conference table. "So, here's what we're going to do. We are going to adjust the lost projections of this quarter and add them to the projections for next quarter. You will meet these next quarterly projections or...."

"You can kiss your jobs good bye," Dr Patterson said.

"You can kiss your jobs good bye," Laurel said as a vein visibly shown on her forehead.

Sam turned to Dr. Patterson. "How did you know she was going to say that?" he asked.

"It's what all inept leaders say when they can't see the connection between their lack of leadership and the lack of performance by their staff."

"You used the word 'inept', pretty calmly," Sam said.

"I can only tell you what I've seen and what's been documented in hundreds of studies done on leadership." Dr. Patterson stated. "Leading by threat or fear only pushes employees toward deception, false results or out the door."

Dr. Patterson explained to Sam that through her years of consulting work, she has provided personal coaching for numerous managers, directors and executive staff that used the 'fear' approach to leadership as their only weapon for ensuring results.

"Sam, do you remember that kid Herbie Stowe from your sixth grade class?"

"Wow, Herbie. Now there's a name I haven't thought about in a long...., wait a minute. How did you know about Herbie?"

"You do remember him, don't you?"

"Yeah, I remember that he was a bully. He was taller than most of us, heavier and always shoving people around. There were always certain kids he'd pick on."

"Why didn't he pick on you?"

"I don't know. At the time he was bigger than me."

"Were you afraid of him?" Dr. Patterson asked.

"Not so he'd know. I never really got in his way."

"What about the time he threatened to get you after school when you refused to give him your Mom's homemade oatmeal cookies that you'd brought with your lunch?"

"Dr. Patterson, this is getting weird. How did you know about that?"

"Why did you refuse?" She asked.

"The cookies weren't his, they were mine. I guess I decided that if we were going to fight over cookies after school, so be it."

"What happened?"

"He changed his mind. He let me off with a warning."

"So, were you really going to fight him over those cookies?"

"Yeah, I guess if I had to."

"Why?" Dr Patterson asked.

"Well, one day it's cookies and the next day it's the keys to your summer home." Sam replied. "I took a stand. Despite his size, I wasn't going to let him push me around."

"Do you see any parallels going on here with Laurel and her staff?"

Sam thought for a moment. "Why should she respect them if they are letting her push them around?" He reflected for another moment. "Now is the time for them to take a stand and make her listen to them."

"What's the worst that can happen?" Dr. Patterson asked.

"The worst has already happened. I suspect half of them will leave the room and head to the Internet to conduct a job search."

"Actually, all four of them did that very thing." Dr. Patterson stated. "You see, Laurel failed to realize that the lull between her leadership and their performance has little to do with their fear of losing a job. It had everything to do with her inability to tap into their creative reservoir. She shackles their performance and then gets angry when they don't move."

"But, this wasn't my issue," Sam stated.

"Not yet, for now it's your lesson," Dr Patterson replied. "Look at the blinds on the window behind Laurel."

The closed blinds kept out the sunlight, but on them Sam read:

- Fear is the opiate of the insecure
- People bring the results they've been unleashed to fulfill
- What happens behind your back says a lot about what you're doing up front
- Delegating to develop talent is far different from dumping to unload tasks

Sam asked, "Do you think Laurel will get those next quarterly results?"

"Not in the manner she expected, Sam." Dr. Patterson said. "But, let's move on."

➤ CHAPTER 10 ➤

Sam and Dr. Patterson stood in the semi-cubed office of Donald Crawford, the forty-something Director of Human Resources, as he conversed with an employee. The closed door discussion was part of the commitment made by Human Resource departments to maintain confidentiality around employee concerns while still serving the needs and goals of the organization. Completely unaware that the conversation had three listeners, the employee, Chana Lundy, rambled on and on about being denied a promotion.

"Mr. Crawford, this is the third time it has happened. That makes me a three time, three strikes loser with no future with the company. I don't think its fair and I'm not going down this easily." Chana said.

Don Crawford had nodded his head a few times just to reassure Chana that he had been listening. When Chana finished talking, Don said. "Chana, we've gone over this before." He opened a folder and flipped through a few pages. "Your evaluations from your manager and peers all describe you as someone who consistently 'Meets Expectations'"

"So, why can't I get promoted?" Chana asked.

As Don began to answer her question, Sam turned to Dr. Patterson.

"Having had to work with her, I know why she can't get promoted."

"Why is that?" Dr. Patterson asked.

"Anybody can meet expectations if they just do their job. Her problem is she takes no initiative. When we worked on a project together, I would assign her a task and she'd complete the task, but she always waited until she was assigned another task. Everyone involved on the project knew all the tasks that needed to be accomplished. I had it all mapped out on a chart complete with timelines. She'd perform the task and wait for me to give her something else to do."

Dr. Patterson motioned toward Don Crawford, "I think he agrees with you."

"...it keeps coming back to this critical piece in your work behavior, Chana," Don said. "Working for this company is not just about doing your job. It also means grabbing something the organization needs to have done and running with it until it's completed. We, along with most organizations call it 'taking initiative'. The times we live in don't allow us to sit and wait for something to happen. Competitive success, internally as well as externally, is really about distinguishing your self from a variety of similar choices. Don't you get it? Eighty percent of the people that work here can meet expectations. There's nothing distinguishing about achieving that goal. The real trick is in knowing how to become part of the high performing ten percent."

"Don't you mean the other twenty percent?" Chana asked.

"No, I meant the high performing ten percent. On the other side of those numbers is the low performing ten percent. We do what we can with those employees, but they rarely stay around for the job, much less a promotion." Don replied.

"But, I've been a good employee. It's not fair that..."

Don interrupted, "What isn't fair, Chana is for you or any employee to think that just because you do a good job at what we pay you to do, that it deserves some special acknowledgement or reward. You want to be considered for a promotion, then stop 'meeting expectations' and move to the next level of performance. How about pursuing the degree that keeps getting mentioned in the feedback comments?"

"I just haven't had time to...." Chana's voice began to fade as Sam thought about what he'd just heard.

"Well, I'll just be…, that's pretty much what he said to me a year ago when I applied for the Director's job currently filled by my boss, Cindy Mitchell." Sam said.

"It's my understanding that he practically ordered you to enroll in the Master's program as part of that 'distinguishing yourself' process."

"Yeah, he…, how did you know that?"

"I believe he said your career had reached a lull and that you really needed to do something that was going to broaden your thinking and infuse you with knowledge to help the organization remain competitive." Dr. Patterson said.

"Yes, he said that, but…"

"Wasn't the only difference between your background and Cindy's background is that she had completed a MBA?"

"On paper we were in a dead heat, but then the Vice President decided to go with the fact that she had a MBA and I only had a BA. It was the hardest feedback for me to hear because I thought his using the MBA as a point of separation was purely subjective."

"It was subjective, and…" Dr. Patterson prodded.

"And, I should have never let him have that as an advantage. Had I gone on and completed my MBA two years earlier like I planned then the only thing he could have said to me is that I didn't get the job because he didn't like me."

"You think that would have been hard to hear?" Dr. Patterson asked.

"I prefer someone not liking me, which I can't control, over something I could have controlled, like having my MBA. Ever since I've been enrolled, I have heard from various sources that the perception around the organization is that I am 'taking initiative' and…" Sam paused, looked over at Dr. Patterson and shook his head. "You are one sly devil."

Dr. Patterson smiled innocently.

"You want me to have this conversation with Chana, don't you?

"She might hear it better from you," Dr. Patterson stated.

"You think so?"

"Who better than you understand what it truly means *to take the lull by the horns?* Read what's written on the wall over Don's desk."

Sam glanced over at the statements written on the wall.

- Passion + Persistence = Pathway to Leadership
- Anyone can be good, Not everyone can be exceptional
- The primary purpose of feedback is to guide change
- Distinctions are a matter of degree

Sam sighed, "I'm getting a headache."

"That's what happens when your brain takes on new knowledge," Dr. Patterson said. "I've saved the best for last. Come along."

⇥ CHAPTER 11 ⇥

In the conference room, down the hall from Sam's office, the latest emergency meeting was being convened by Sam's Director, Cindy Mitchell. As the Director of Divisional Planning, one of Cindy's many responsibilities was to ensure the proper use of organizational resources and hold her division accountable for meeting the goals set by the organization. The eight people in attendance included Sam and the other managers that reported directly to Cindy.

"Oh no, not back here. Do I have to relive this nightmare?" Sam asked.

"You might hear things differently this time," Dr. Patterson replied. "Pay attention to the interaction going on between Cindy and the group."

Sam watched as Cindy talked about the recent information that came out of the corporate office. She was frequently interrupted with questions about the mental achievements of the corporate staff. Some of the managers were demanding that Cindy be a lot more supportive of them and confront the corporate staff with the reality of what they were up against. Others sniped at Cindy or each other, and pushed the 'doom and gloom' perspective while voicing their anger at another round of cuts.

"It's not very pretty," Sam said to Dr. Patterson.

"Do you mean the information or the group behavior?" Dr. Patterson asked.

Sam didn't answer, but watched closely as the meeting became more intense. Cindy showed the data from the last quarterly reports, explained the recent downturn in the market and tried to solicit ideas from the group on other things that could be done. In the end, she was unwavering on the issue of cutbacks in staff.

"We're just going to have to find ways to do more with less." Cindy stated

"That has got to be one phrase I am tired of hearing," Sam said to Dr. Patterson.

"I don't think Cindy found much joy in making the statement," Dr. Patterson said. "But, here comes the good part."

Sam watched as he made the comment to Cindy, "How am I supposed to get it done when I will be minus three more staff members?"

And as she had previously stated, Cindy said, "You'll just have to find a way." Sam closed his eyes, thinking about what he'd just seen and what Cindy had said. In that moment, Sam began to realize a number of things about the day and that he was now sitting at a table on the outside patio of his favorite restaurant. Dr Patterson sat in the seat opposite to Sam, gazing at the crisp bluish green river that gently passed in the background. "Any thoughts, Sam?" she asked.

"I guess the day was a little more complex than even I realized." Sam admitted.

"Or a lot simpler than was presented." Dr. Patterson stated.

The faces and events that made up the day raced through Sam's thoughts as if set in motion by a pistol shot. Each face and event was vividly recreated for his analysis and reflection. He'd been given a chance to look back on the day without having to relive each moment. He saw his own conduct, seemingly magnified, by the events in which he was participant.

"I can see where I made a lot of mistakes," Sam admitted.

"They weren't mistakes, Sam. They were missed opportunities. These are the kinds of opportunities that are prevalent in organizations on a daily basis, but are rarely addressed because they seem larger than they are or so insignificant that they don't merit attention. So these opportunities just pass right on by and who knows how much profit is lost because no one is willing to take the lull by the horns."

"Before I give you my thoughts on what I've seen, may I ask you a question?"

"Feel free," Dr. Patterson said.

"Have you ever had occasion to take the lull by the horns?"

Dr. Patterson smiled. It wasn't the first time one of her graduate students wanted to know the extent to which she has actually practiced what she preached. She knew it came with the turf when teaching working practitioners in a graduate program.

"My first teaching assignment," she started, "wasn't given to me by an academic department, but was lying dormant in the institutional bowels of an administrative department in the university. I worked as an administrator and was interested in teaching, but none of the departments were interested in taking on a new PhD that worked in administration. So, one day I was looking through the responsibilities of our department when I noticed that there was an undergraduate education course that was under our jurisdiction, but hadn't been taught in over twenty years. Turns out, it was a two-credit, pass-no grade course that was originally offered to as a training opportunity for students wanting to get involved in student government. I asked my Director if we had any plans for this course, he assured me that we hadn't. I told him I'd like to do something with the course. He didn't object, in fact, he said, "See what you can do with it." So, I developed a syllabus, advertised the course to a few student groups and the following semester, after a twenty year absence, I was teaching a student leadership course to thirty-five students. Now, I will cut to the chaise. A year later, our department offered several sections of that course and it became a revenue generator for the department. Twenty years later, that course is now in an academic department, generating revenue. Now, at the time I couldn't tell you the significance of that experience. It didn't crystallize until years later when I was faced with a similar situation at a Health Care company working as a Project Analyst. Since then, I use that experience as a model whenever I see an opportunity just sitting there waiting to be handled. Most of the time, I don't even ask 'if I can', I just state that 'I will'. I've found that 95% of the time, I encounter no resistance. Do you know why?"

"Yeah, who wants to stop an employee who wants to do more work?" Sam said.

"That's part of it. The other part is that a leader with any savvy would rather applaud your initiative around a failure, than reward your lack of effort around a success."

"So, you see a lull as...."

"...an unrealized opportunity just waiting for a leader." Dr. Patterson added.

"In looking back on the day, it seems that I had a number of them." Sam stated.

"You're not alone," Dr Patterson said. "Look at your menu."

Sam opened the large laminated covered menu and read contents on the inside:

+ A good leader will see a solution or an opportunity in any problem
+ Lulls prevent an organization from being completely connected to its profitably creative side
+ It's not enough to know, you have to do
+ What passes in front of you is life, what sits in front of you is opportunity

Sam closed the menu, looked at Dr. Patterson and asked, "So, when does all of this start to make sense?"

Dr. Patterson smiled, leaned forward and said, "The moment you decide to wake up."

CHAPTER 12

"Wake up, Sam," the voice said as he was gently nudged.

Startled, Sam opened his eyes and saw Dr. Patterson standing in front of him. He quickly looked around the room, finally realizing that he was in the faculty lounge and had fallen asleep on the sofa.

"Dr Patterson?"

"Yes, and you're Sam Brown, a confused graduate student coming out of a much needed nap on evening when he is not supposed to be here."

Sam slid toward the edge of the couch, rubbed his eyes and stared at Dr. Patterson. "How long have I been asleep?"

Dr. Patterson glanced at her watch. "I'd say about ten minutes. I was tempted to let you rest a little longer but the lounge will be buzzing with activity pretty soon."

Sam stood up, never taking his eyes off Dr. Patterson. He squinted, furrowed his eyebrows and then stood wide eyed.

"Sam, are you okay?" Dr. Patterson asked. "You're giving me the oddest stare."

"I just had the most fascinating dream, and you were in it."

"Oh really," Dr Patterson said. "Would I be alarmed at the details of this dream?"

"Not in the way you'd think," Sam replied. "Let's just say that in my dream, you forced me to rethink some things I went through today."

"You're not advancing a creative justification for sleeping through my lectures, are you?"

Smiling, Sam picked up his briefcase and said, "No, nothing like that. Well, I guess I'll head home. We can try this again tomorrow night."

"I still have a little time if you want to talk," Dr. Patterson said.

Sam stopped, turned around and said: "We already have, Dr. Patterson. We already have,"

⇥ EPILOGUE ⇤

Dr. Patterson watched Sam as he eased down the long corridor that led to the front doors and into the parking lot.

She smiled.

She turned, walked back to the faculty area and sat down in front of the flat screen computer on the desk in her office. She pointed and clicked onto a file labeled 'The List'. The file opened, revealing a long list of names, listed by 'time of encounter'. She scrolled down the list until she came to Sam Brown's name next to an unchecked box.

She sighed, pointed to the empty box and tapped a small 'x' into the unmarked area. She tapped the current date in the space next to his name followed by a smiling happy face. She glanced at the counter in the top left hand corner of the screen and noted the number.

She smiled, and said. "That's a lot of names. Let me see whose next."

CPSIA information can be obtained
at www.ICGtesting.com
Printed in the USA
FSOW02n1343010317
31407FS